Holding the Heavy Stuff

Holding the Heavy Stuff

Making space for critical thoughts and painful emotions

Ben Sedley

ROBINSON

ROBINSON

First published in Great Britain in 2025 by Robinson

Copyright © Ben Sedley, 2025

Book design by: Catherine Adam, wonderbird.nz
Illustrations by: Kalos Chan

1 3 5 7 9 10 8 6 4 2

The moral right of the author has been asserted.

All rights reserved.

No part of this publication may be reproduced, stored in a retrieval system, or transmitted, in any form, or by any means, without the prior permission in writing of the publisher, nor be otherwise circulated in any form of binding or cover other than that in which it is published and without a similar condition including this condition being imposed on the subsequent purchaser.

A CIP catalogue record for this book is available from the British Library.

ISBN: 978-1-47215-001-1

Printed and bound in Great Britain by Clays Ltd, Elcograf S.p.A.

Papers used by Robinson are from well-managed forests and other responsible sources.

Robinson
An imprint of
Little, Brown Book Group
Carmelite House
50 Victoria Embankment
London EC4Y 0DZ

An Hachette UK Company
www.hachette.co.uk
www.littlebrown.co.uk

The authorised representative
in the EEA is
Hachette Ireland
8 Castlecourt Centre
Dublin 15, D15 XTP3, Ireland
(email: info@hbgi.ie)

For Ben, Ngahuia, Ekara and Paikea

Contents

Chapter 1: **The Heavy Stuff** **4**
    Exercise: Being here now 11

Chapter 2: **The Heavy Stuff** *Gets Heavier* **12**

Chapter 3: **Holding the Heavy Stuff** *with Presence* **24**
    Exercise: Connecting to your breath 26
    Exercise: Connecting to your senses 28
    Exercise: Other ways to connect 29
    Exercise: Connecting with all of yourself 32

Chapter 4: **Holding the Heavy Stuff** *with Compassion* **36**
    Exercise: Flows of compassion 48
    Exercise: Compassionate voice 52

Chapter 5: **Holding the Heavy Stuff** *with Curiosity* **60**
    Exercise: Noticing from multiple angles 64
    Exercise: I am… 68
    Exercise: Observing images 72
    Exercise: Getting to know your emotional discomfort 80
    Exercise: Noticing more than your mind tells you 82

Chapter 6: **Holding the Heavy Stuff** *with Purpose* **86**
    Exercise: The perfect coffee 90
    Exercise: My own personal purpose 91
    Exercise: Stepping 97

Chapter 7: **Holding the Heavy Stuff** *with Support* **104**

Further Reading **118**

Acknowledgements **119**

This book is not the answer

Sorry. I haven't even met you. I haven't heard your story. How can I write a book that solves your problems – a book that is just right for you? This book won't make you happier, wiser or more popular. It's just a book.

In fact, there are over 100,000 self-help books on sale. None of them are exactly right for you either.

In here you'll find ideas that help me and some of the people I work with in my clinical psychology practice. I hope some of them will help you too.

Perhaps you struggle to live the life you want or are holding too much heavy stuff. You feel weighed down by painful feelings such as sadness, worry or shame, or you feel held back by self-criticism. As you read the ideas in this book, maybe you'll try them and perhaps that will help you move your life towards the people, things and ideas that matter to you.

No book (or person or podcast or lifehack) is the perfect answer. But trying out ideas, taking steps, doing things . . . **that is the beginning of something new**.

Holding the Heavy Stuff

There are lots of *external* things that cause pain and weigh us down. Awful things like wars, environmental disasters, prejudice, violence, viruses, health crises and poverty.

And then some pain is *internal* – mean thoughts, uncomfortable emotions, graphic images, loud urges, heartbreaking memories. But **having** internal pain is not the problem; it's part of being human. How we **respond** to internal pain can be the problem. Our response changes how much the pain hurts us. Our response determines how much control the pain has over us and either constricts us or energises us to move towards the life that matters to us.

Paradoxically, the more we try to fight internal pain, the more we have it. Instead of struggling against it, I want to share with you a different approach. We'll look at ways to **hold the heavy stuff** and carry it with us as we go where we want to go.

First, we'll look at what I mean by **the heavy stuff**, with examples of different struggles that people face. Then we'll notice things that make **the heavy stuff heavier**. Our responses to our pain and our understandable dislike of being in pain often lead us to do things that inadvertently increase how stuck we feel and how much it hurts.

Instead, we're going to **hold the heavy stuff *with presence***, one breath at a time. We'll learn to **hold the heavy stuff *with compassion***, observing the power of love and a caring internal voice. We'll **hold the heavy stuff *with curiosity***, taking a step back from our thoughts and feelings to see them as they really are, rather than what they tell us they are. This will allow us to **hold the heavy stuff *with purpose***, deliberately choosing to move in the directions that we care about. Finally, we'll **hold the heavy stuff *with support***, identifying other people and things who can help as we go on our path.

As you'll see in the examples coming up, **Holding the Heavy Stuff** is for anyone who has struggled with self-doubts or mean thoughts about themselves and then found it difficult to move their life forward.

It is for people who feel overwhelmed or consumed by worries about the future, or find themselves stuck reliving moments from their past.

It is for those who have days, weeks or months when sadness takes over and getting through each hour feels challenging.

It is for those who can't imagine life getting better as the world gets worse.

It is for people who feel dumped on or knocked off track.

It is for all of us who face tragedy and difficulty and feel weighed down.

It is also for the friends, partners and family members who care about the people described above.

So if you're holding heavy stuff or are supporting someone holding heavy stuff, I wrote this for you, and I hope you will find something useful in the pages ahead.

Chapter One.
The Heavy Stuff

Everywhere **Erin** looks, she finds things that worry her. It feels like friends take forever to respond to her messages. Her family makes comments that replay in her head long after the conversation ends. She spends hours wondering if strangers on the street think she's as weird as she feels. Everyone else around her seems to manage well, but for Erin, even simple tasks feel overwhelming.

On Sundays, her mind plays endless scenarios of how her upcoming week at work might go wrong. Each night she lies in bed, reliving every mistake she made that day at work. Her body is tense, her heart feels like it will beat out of her chest, her breath never slows down, her mind is always racing.

Ever since **Jeong's** relationship ended, he feels weighed down by everything. Moving feels hard, thinking even harder, and the meanest thoughts about what a terrible person he is repeat endlessly in his head. He feels constantly tired but still can't sleep. His appetite is non-existent; even thinking about eating feels like a chore. He doesn't enjoy watching sport like he used to and he can't imagine playing a friendly game of football with the boys any more. There are days when he can't stop crying; other days he wishes he could cry just to feel something. Those numb days are the worst.

No one really understood how horrible **Nicki's** stepfather was to her when she was growing up. Looking back, she wasn't even sure whether his fists or his words were more harmful. Often, the most painful part came when her mother told her that he didn't really mean it, or that he would change. It's been years since Nicki had any contact with her stepfather, but his legacy of threats and criticism remains in the way she doubts her every move, the way she sometimes feels unsteady or freezes. She can even hear his cruel words echo in the way she talks to herself when she screws up.

Even though her boss has always been supportive, she still avoids volunteering for tasks or allowing herself to stand out in any way. She feels so lonely but avoids getting too close to anyone, knowing it will only be a matter of time before each friend hurts her or abandons her. Relationships don't tend to last long; it's hard to relax around someone when you're bracing yourself for the pain that will eventually come. Sometimes it's easier to bring on the inevitable fight.

Emptiness is the closest word **Omar** finds to describe how they are feeling. They have the job they'd always hoped to get. Their friends from law school would be so impressed with where they ended up. But they don't feel impressed with themselves, they just feel bored. They win a case, get praised by the partners, but so what?

Days turn into months, and things just feel blah. What's the point of having a good salary if you don't have anything you feel like spending it on? Since COVID, they continue to work from home and hardly ever leave the house or see anyone.

Dalia sits in the bathroom at university. She calls herself pathetic, a crybaby. What possible right does she have to find this transition to university so hard? She comes from a good family, has a place to live and food to eat. Others have it so much worse than she does. She tells herself again just to get over it and toughen up. Yet, despite telling herself to stop crying and feel better, she doesn't feel any better at all. In fact, she feels worse. Pathetic.

Tony feels good. His life is good. His friends struggle with stressful jobs, difficult relationships, money worries, new diets or exercise regimes. But Tony doesn't worry about any of that. He spends his days smoking weed, gaming, eating nachos and watching Netflix. In school he was a top student and a good runner. These days he feels short of breath walking to the corner store. But who needs to go out, right? You can order anything to be delivered to you now. At times, he wonders if there is more to life than this, but he has found that getting high is a great way of quietening that voice.

Have you had similar experiences to the people I've described?

You may feel overwhelmed, depressed, anxious, frustrated, ashamed, confused or just plain sick of it all. You might be constantly stuck in your head, feeling tortured by unsupportive thoughts. Maybe you have lost sight of the directions you want your life to go in.

Or your experiences may differ greatly from the people I've described. These are incredibly strange times, with pandemics, recessions and political uncertainty leaving so many of us feeling alone and stuck and trying to make sense of things that weren't imaginable a decade ago.

This book is not a substitute for therapy. I hope the ideas here resonate with you, but it's still not the same as sitting in a room with someone who listens to you alone and helps you navigate your own challenging experiences.

Please listen to your own heart as well as what I write here.

Only you will know if the ideas in this book are the ones you need for your particular struggles at this particular time. In these pages, I will make suggestions. Please try them and listen to your own experience. **If the ideas here feel helpful for you, then use them**. If they aren't what you need right now, then please think about ways to adapt them so they work for you, or keep looking for other strategies.

The book draws on ideas from **acceptance and commitment therapy (ACT)**, the therapy I use in my psychology practice and for myself. The core idea is that trying to get away from our thoughts and feelings actually leads us to feeling more stuck and distressed. So instead, we will discuss ways to make space for these painful inner experiences and then use our limited time and energy to move towards the people, things and ideas that really matter to us. Put simply, we will learn how to hold the heavy stuff and carry it in meaningful directions.

We will also use some ideas from **compassion focused therapy (CFT)** so that, as we take steps forward, we can draw on our own strength, courage, kindness and wisdom.

Noticing

Making changes in life takes practice. It doesn't matter how many self-help books you read, how many therapists you see or how many positive things you tell yourself. **Change comes from looking around you and then moving**. You need to take steps. Even really small steps can bring you closer to where you want to be.

This book contains many exercises. Several of them involve awareness of your breath, as your breath is one of the most reliable and powerful ways to turn your attention back to where you are right now. Where you are right now might not be pleasant or comfortable; it might hurt a lot. But it's the only place you can learn from in this moment.

When you come to an exercise in this book, pause and give it a go. This will give you a chance to learn from your own immediate experience, rather than just learning from my words.

Oh look, here comes an exercise now:

EXERCISE:
Being here now

Sit comfortably in your seat; notice what it feels like to be sitting right here, right now. Notice your feet touching the ground . . .

Notice the top of your head . . .

And everything in between.

Breathe in.

Feel the breath enter your body, feel your lungs expand, feel your chest rise.

As you breathe out, notice the breath leaving your body. Feel the movement in your stomach and chest. Notice the breath as it comes out of your mouth or nose.

Follow your breath in and out of your body at least three more times. Don't try to control or change your breath. Just let it do what it needs to do to nourish and nurture you.

Welcome to this moment. The only moment you are in right now.

What did you notice as you observed your breath and where you are right now? Maybe you noticed all the noise getting in the way, even in such a simple exercise. Maybe you felt an urge to avoid that noise. This desire to avoid makes the heavier stuff feel heavier.

Chapter Two.

The Heavy Stuff Gets Heavier

Imagine that one day your car breaks down and you have to call emergency services from the side of the road. You call and say, 'My car has broken down,' and before you give any more details about where you are or what happened to the car, the person on the phone starts giving advice about how to fix it.

Their recommendations wouldn't be helpful unless they first understood where you were and what had happened to your car.

Unfortunately, when it comes to painful emotions, we often get bombarded with suggestions from people who don't comprehend our situation and what we're struggling with.

So many things affect our ability to live the life we had hoped for. There are so many different reasons why we might be holding heavy stuff.

Some of us started life in a supportive environment, some of us didn't.

Some of us had parents who loved us to bits, but still weren't able to provide what we needed.

Some of us grew up in difficult places or difficult times.

Some of us had to start over in a new place.

Some of us had the kind of brains that they value at school. Some of us had to survive school and then figure out who we are and how we learn best.

Some of us found friends, partners, bosses and co-workers who were safe and respectful. Some of us didn't.

Some of us enjoyed the slower pace of being at home during the pandemic. Some of us were stuck somewhere unsafe at that time, in an unpredictable world.

Some of us had people who needed so much from us that there wasn't time for ourselves.

Some of us were left alone.

Some of us experienced bullying, discrimination or illness.

Some of us have been attacked or hurt – physically, verbally, sexually, emotionally. Some of us were ignored or made to feel like we didn't matter.

Each of us had to make sense of the particular world that we grew up in.

Some of us were given the space we needed to explore the world and learn its rules. We felt secure enough to observe variations, inconsistencies or exceptions to any rules we noticed.

Some of us were told to follow rules no matter what.

Some of us felt safe enough to look around and figure out what was needed each new day.

Some of us had to keep our head down and our eyes forward at all times, and we had to keep following old rules in order not to be hurt. Often those rules hurt too.

All of us tried to develop ways to avoid our sadness and worries. These strategies may have helped us for a short while, or they may still be useful.

Some of us learned that words, including thoughts, can be magical and can be played with or held lightly.

Some of us were taught that words can cause pain and that there will be consequences for saying or even thinking the wrong thing.

Some of us got to learn who we are, and discovered words to describe ourselves and how we feel.

Some of us were taught that it's wrong to be kind to ourselves or that we don't deserve the love and respect that others have.

All of us have the right to feel the way we do and all of us have the right to try to change what we do if it's not working for us.

When we talk about finding a path that works for you, we need to remember that everyone starts from a different place with a different history, body, culture and family.

Sometimes ideas that sound simple can still be difficult to do or require lots of practice.

There will be many challenges and unexpected twists along the way. You are going to move at a different speed to others around you, and wanting to move faster than you're able to won't make it easier to progress quickly.

If where you are and how you're currently living doesn't feel right for you, then now is the time to take steps.

So, as we discuss ways to hold the heavy stuff and move in your chosen direction, be kind to yourself and be respectful of your own experiences.

These steps may not always be the comfortable or easy option, yet you can be generous to yourself as you move forward. Approach these ideas with compassionate courage.

Unfortunately, these differences in experience are constantly forgotten. Instead, you are told that being happy and successful is easy. People may have said things like that to you. They may have seen you in pain and told you to 'get over it' or 'be tougher' or 'think differently'. Maybe they said that the heavy stuff isn't really that heavy and you just need to get on with things.

You may have listened to experts talking about how they are successful because they thought positively or visualised their success, with the unspoken implication that, if you have negative thoughts or images, you won't be successful. You may have seen ads where everyone is happy all the time because they're using the right products or adopting the right mindset.

All this advice comes from where the speaker is sitting, rather than them understanding your situation.

We live in a world that gives a very strong message that if you're not happy all the time, something is wrong with you. We get this message through friends and family telling us to cheer up or not to worry so much. We get this message through self-help influencers, successful business people, sports people and musicians. We get this message from social media, where people get to curate the way their life is presented to tell a particular story. Based on all these influences, it is easy to think that if you are not successful it must be your fault, because you just didn't want it badly enough.

'Don't worry about it'

'Don't dwell on the bad stuff'

'Don't think so negatively'

It is confusing when the advice you're given is telling you what not to do, rather than what to do. It's especially confusing when people who are giving this advice don't understand where you're coming from and where you're trying to get to.

But you don't like being in pain, so you do all you can to keep away uncomfortable feelings. Feelings like:

Sadness **Shame**

Guilt *Confusion*

Worry Frustration

Trust ***Hate***

Doubt **Anger**

Embarrassment *Despair*

Loneliness *Love**

*yes, unfortunately, even love can fit in this category sometimes

Keeping away from emotions that you don't want can take a lot of work.

Sometimes it can be a full-time job.

In order to keep away from sadness or worry, you might:

Avoid things
Try to have only positive thoughts
Drink alcohol
Overeat
Lie
Self-harm
Exercise
Go to therapy
Use medication
Keep your distance from people
Take risks
Stay in familiar places or routines
Hide feelings
Put yourself down
Meditate
Mask your true self
Reject people
Try to control your thoughts
Blame yourself
Make excuses
Have unsafe sex
Think about suicide
Pick fights
Stay in bed
Get wasted
Stay on social media
Stay off social media

I'm sure you've noticed that some of those things on the list are obviously negative and 'bad' things to do, but some of the other actions sound like 'good' things to do, and some could go either way.

But right now we're not talking about 'good' or 'bad', we're asking: *Do these things help you get rid of thoughts and feelings you don't want?* If you're doing those things to eliminate unwanted thoughts or feelings, then they are all effective in the short term, yet none of them permanently eliminate internal pain.

If you're drinking to erase sad memories and nasty thoughts about yourself, then it will work really well short term. Long term, not so much.

If you're going to the gym because you value being fit, then it can be a really effective way to achieve that goal. But if you're going to the gym to rid yourself of self-critical thoughts or shame, then you'll probably find that the feelings don't stay away for long, and even that break from them requires a fight. And that fighting consumes a whole lot of precious energy that you could be using in other ways.

While you're exerting effort to avoid feeling, thinking or remembering something, you don't have much brain power or energy left to focus on living the life you want to have right now.

We might also follow rules or ideas that we hope will keep us safe:

If it's not perfect, don't let anyone see it.

No one cares what I think.

Others' needs are always more important than mine.

If something goes wrong, it's my fault.

Others can't be trusted.

Conflict must be avoided at all costs.

Thinking something bad is as bad as doing it.

No one else has thoughts like these.

I deserved it.

If I'm kind to myself, I won't achieve what I want to achieve.

I'm broken.

Your rules and beliefs about yourself originated from your experiences and the messages that others directly or indirectly gave you. This includes the beliefs that sound cruel and the rules that make it harder to do what you want to do.

Most beliefs and rules developed because, at some point, they were needed to help you stay safe.

Perhaps you were rejected when you spoke up, or criticised when you tried new things. Maybe blaming yourself felt safer than acknowledging that the adults in your life weren't doing what they should have been doing. Maybe you witnessed disagreements or conflict that resulted in real pain.

These rules and beliefs that served you earlier in your life may not be the ones that will help you thrive right now. It could be time to notice that you are here now in this moment, and you're able to hold these thoughts with flexibility and compassion.

Chapter Three.
Holding the Heavy Stuff *with* Presence

Our minds are excellent problem-solving machines. They take all the information we've learned growing up and use it to make decisions about the best thing to do right now. This can be a really helpful, and sometimes life-saving, skill.

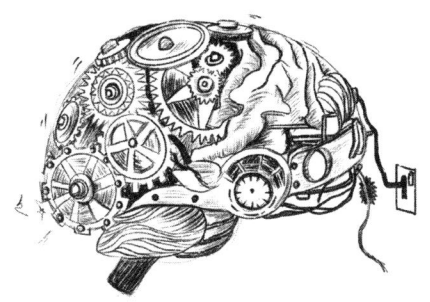

You don't need to experience every possible dangerous thing in the world to know what is dangerous. Your mind can draw on everything you've personally experienced, combine it with things you've learned from others, and imagine possible futures where things might go wrong, then plan out ways to avoid those things. Some of these connections are logical, such as knowing to drive more slowly after almost getting killed while speeding. Other connections are less logical, such as trying to avoid red things because of a near-fatal accident in a red car. When brains are feeling under threat, emotions and instincts guide them, rather than calm, flexible logic.

Often we navigate the current world using rules that we learned at other times in our life, even when there are important differences between now and then and the current situation would be better managed with a different solution. For example, if you were frequently laughed at in school for getting answers wrong, you might not answer questions in a new setting, even when you're now in a room full of supportive people. Or if you've been hurt in a relationship before, you might find it hard to trust your current partner, even when there are significant differences in how this new partner treats you compared to your past partner. The rule '*I mustn't take risks*' might have been really useful when you were surrounded by people who punished you for getting it wrong, but it might be getting in the way now as you contemplate changing career.

These rules are helpful, except when they're not. The trick is to notice when they are helpful and when they're holding you back. But to figure that out, you need to know where you are right now.

Not where your mind tells you that you are, but where you really are.

So how do you know where you are? Yup, you guessed it, you start with your breath.

EXERCISE:
Connecting to your breath

Have you ever noticed that when you're really stressed, people often remind you to take a breath? That's because your breath is happening right now. When you're stressed, you're probably busy thinking about where you've been or all the things that are coming in the future.

Even though you've been breathing every minute of your life, it's still helpful to practise breathing. Take slow, deliberate breaths and focus on what it feels like to breathe in ... and what it feels like to breathe out.

Find a quiet, safe place to sit and breathe in for a count of five, hold for two, then out for a count of five. If five is too long for you, then breathe in and out to the count of four or even three.

Observe as the breath passes around the discomfort – the sadness, the tight chest or whatever else might be there. Although it is unpleasant, it is still possible to breathe. Through this simple observation, you can see that there is more to you than the discomfort, even when the discomfort hurts a lot.

Let's expand this exercise further. Pause reading and take three focused breaths. With each breath, notice what it feels like to breathe in and to breathe out.

When other thoughts try to distract you – and they will – rather than arguing with them or trying to get rid of them, gently notice that you're having another thought and then return your focus to your breath. You'll probably need to do this over and over and over.

What did you notice as you focused on these breaths? Was there room for the breath as well as the judgements, distractions and emotions?

Now to expand this even further. Set a timer on your phone for three minutes and spend this time noticing what it feels like to breathe in and breathe out. Or find an app or online video that leads you through a breathing exercise.

Every time thoughts or feelings try to distract you, notice that the thought or feeling is there, and return your focus to your breath. The goal isn't to empty your mind or stop thinking. The aim is only to notice the breath, perceive the internal noise, and gently bring your focus back to your breath.

If turning your attention to your breath is difficult – if your breath feels shallow or uncomfortable, or if you're reminded of other times when breathing was hard or felt unsafe – then notice that with compassion and do what you're able to do and no more than that.

What did you notice when you did that?

Did you find that your mind kept trying to distract you, urging you to focus on other things – stuff from the past, things you 'should' be doing instead of this or 'should' be doing next? Maybe there were even judgements about the exercise you were doing – whether you were doing it right or whether you should be doing it at all.

Our minds have evolved to judge, plan and problem-solve, so when your mind does those things, it's simply doing its job. Your job is to notice that your mind is handing you a lot of thoughts and realise that there's room inside of you for those thoughts, while you still turn your attention back to your breath.

Your breath is an anchor to help you notice *where* and *when* you are right now. You can observe all the thoughts that show up, including all those rules about how you should be and how you should feel. You can notice all those feelings that emerge and recognise that there's room inside you for them. When you create the space to notice these thoughts and feelings, you give yourself the chance to choose what behaviours might be the most effective in your current situation.

EXERCISE:
Connecting to your senses

You can also use your senses to help you know where you are right now, which is often a different place from where your mind tells you that you should be.

A common exercise people use to help their senses reconnect them to the present moment is **5-4-3-2-1**:

Notice **five** things you can see ... What colours, shapes, objects and shadows do you observe?

Notice **four** things you can hear ... How many sounds can you hear right now? What sounds are nearby? What sounds are further away?

Notice **three** things you can touch ... What can you feel right now? Notice contact points. Are your feet touching the ground? Can you feel the chair you're sitting on? What are your hands touching? Where can you feel the air touching your body?

Notice **two** things you can smell ... You may not have words for the smells, but what can you notice as you breathe in?

Notice **one** thing you can taste ... Lick your lips. What tastes are there? Are there specific tastes from recent food or drink? Or are there vaguer tastes without specific words or connections?

What did you notice as you did that?
If you're anything like me, you might have observed your mind being full of judgements about everything you were noticing with one of your senses. Minds love to constantly judge, compare, predict, reminisce and problem-solve. Even while your mind was making that noise, were you able to allow your senses just to let you know where you are right now?

EXERCISE:
Other ways to connect

There are many other ways you can use one or more of your senses to bring you back to the present.

When you're drinking your tea or coffee, feel the warmth of the cup, watch the steam, breathe in the smell and, of course, let your taste buds really enjoy the flavours.

When you're listening to music, notice all the different components. What is each instrument doing? What does it feel like when it goes quieter or louder or maybe speeds up or slows down?

When you're out and about, what shapes, colours and patterns can you see? If it's a familiar place, can you see something you've not noticed before? If it's a new place, what are some things that stand out? Is it something surprising? If it's in nature, how many shades of green can you see?

When you're in the shower or cleaning your teeth, what are all your senses telling you? Allow your kinaesthetic sense (body feelings) to come alive. Where can you feel the water? What position is your body in? What can you smell and taste?

You can also connect to the present by connecting with others and yourself.

Connecting with another person: Is there someone in your life who you truly care about, not because you want something from them, but just because they are who they are? Talk to them, listen to them, hug them, phone them or send them a message. Be sensitive to their needs. Connect to them simply because they matter to you.

Connecting with yourself: How might you connect with yourself? Spend a moment listening to yourself, making yourself a cup of tea, hugging yourself or caring for yourself. Be sensitive to your needs. Connect with yourself simply because you matter to you.

EXERCISE:
Connecting with all of yourself

I invite you to bring to mind an instance when you tried to do something for the first time or learned a new skill. Ideally, think of something that you can now do with more confidence. Maybe it was learning to drive, bake or perform a job-related skill. Notice what it felt like as you learned that skill. What was happening in your mind as you figured out each component of the skill? What was happening in your body? What's happening right now as you remember what it felt like to learn that new skill?

Now, think of a recent time when you performed that same skill with more confidence. Maybe by now the skill feels so routine that it's hard to even notice that you're doing it, or maybe it's something that you can enjoy doing without having to focus closely on each aspect. What was happening in your mind as you completed the skill with confidence? What was happening in your body as you acted skilfully and confidently? What's happening right now as you remember feeling confident and competent?

What happens as you switch between those two memories? Can you notice that neither one of those moments in time defines you? Neither memory 'is' you; they are both simply experiences you've had. And notice that right now you can observe these and all other moments in your life — the times you did well, the times you said the right thing, the times you messed up, the times you acted in ways that you're now embarrassed by.

Notice that you can be here now observing all those memories, and none of those memories define you. You are more than your worst days. You are more than your best days, too. You can notice all these emotions, sensations, self-judgements, memories and thoughts. You can even observe the part of you that is observing all these thoughts and feelings. There is a part of you that is outside all of these internal experiences, a part that can choose which emotions and judgements will help you move towards your goals, and which ones might just need to come along for the ride as you live a valued life.

What was it like to observe that you are more than any thought, any feeling, any story about yourself? What difference has it made to your day to spend a few minutes noticing where you are? Connecting to the present moment won't directly change how you feel, but this increased awareness can open up the possibility that you might choose to do something different or treat yourself differently.

Even though her stepfather was out of her life, **Nicki** could hear his cold, menacing voice and braced herself for the verbal abuse or physical assaults that used to come next. While at work, trying to focus on a project, half her brain stayed on the lookout for people coming to criticise her. Her logical brain reminded her that her boss was supportive, but when he gave her feedback on how to improve her reports, she felt stuck in her fight, flight or freeze mode. She felt caught between wanting to quit her job and dissociating, unable to take in a word he said.

Nicki knew she had a meeting with her boss coming up, so she spent a few moments preparing. She put her feet on the ground and noticed what it felt like to be in the present, touching the ground. She took three slow, deliberate breaths, noticing what it felt like to breathe in and breathe out. She looked around and engaged all of her senses to let that scared child part of her know that she was now an adult and not facing the person who had hurt her. During the meeting, several times she felt the protective parts of herself trying to pull her mind away, but she chose to bring her attention back to her breath and then to what was happening in the room. She used her compassionate voice to remind herself that she was here now and that she had got this.

Nicki still went to therapy to process the trauma she had been through in the past, but in between sessions, her breath and compassionate voice helped her know that she was in the present, not still back there trying to survive.

Chapter Four.

Holding the Heavy Stuff *with* Compassion

Life is stressful.

Life is stressful on those really hard days when deadlines, pressures and expectations build up more than usual.

But life is stressful on all the other days too. Even on those ordinary days when you're just trying to pay the bills, support your loved ones, complete life chores, take care of yourself and maintain an interest in the world.

Every minute of every day, multiple issues demand your attention in real life or online, telling you about things you need to worry about or deal with. There's no time to catch your breath and just be. Before you even get out of bed, the news has told you about people dying around the world, your phone has listed a range of challenges and issues your online friends are dealing with, and your brain has thrown an impossibly long to-do list at you.

You work really hard to keep up with this constant bombardment of threats, needs, dilemmas and conflicting demands on your time. Your mind offers a number of solutions to help you with all this pressure. It can encourage you to think more about the dangers around you, which can lead to doom-scrolling or spiralling in unhelpful directions. It can suggest procrastination, allowing you to avoid thinking about what needs to be done. Your internal voice can try to bully you, putting you down until you're achieving more. Or it can point out that you're trying to do too much and offer the seemingly *helpful* solution of dropping something, and then every time suggest that the thing that you drop is looking after yourself. This might lead you to sleep less, eat worse, reduce exercise or give up on those moments where you pause to catch your breath. Consequently, you feel worse about yourself, more stressed and more hopeless about ever getting through all the things on your plate.

Why is it so much easier to prioritise caring for others over ourselves?

In this chapter, we're going to talk about the importance of **compassion** and look at ways to cultivate an internal compassionate voice.

I know, I've just drawn your attention to all the things you've already got to do, and my solution is to give you more to do. And this is still worth doing. Because it helps. Evidence shows that increasing self-compassion can help you to look after what really matters to you and have more resilience to manage stress.

HOLDING THE HEAVY STUFF WITH COMPASSION

Do you spend much time watching cats? I often watch the cats that live on my street, especially my neighbour's cat Grey Wolf. Most of the time, Grey Wolf explores the world, looking for food, taunting birds or chasing balls of string. I like to think he is having amazing adventures in his mind, imagining himself as a great warrior or brave explorer, even when he's just playing in the backyard. His body tenses with anticipation and excitement, his mind focused on the rewards and fun to be had. His **resource-seeking system** is activated.

Suddenly, Grey Wolf hears a dog bark or an unexpected noise, and he stops doing whatever he was doing. His senses sharpen, his claws pop out, his heart rate increases and he prepares for whatever threat might come his way. His mind anticipates possible threats – a dangerous dog, that loud neighbourhood kid, a thunderstorm. This is his **threat system**.

Then the threat passes, and Grey Wolf continues exploring. But then he walks into a sunspot. He cancels his plans for the rest of the day and enjoys the warmth and calm. His body relaxes, breath and heart rate slow, and his **soothing system** activates. Grey Wolf also loves activating his soothing system by curling up on the knee of people he loves. He purrs happily as he gets strokes and cuddles from his gentle, caring owner.

All animals have these three regulation systems: a resource-seeking system, a threat system and a soothing system. Humans have these three systems too, but unfortunately it's never that straightforward with humans. We tend to complicate things in ways that don't always work for our bodies.

As our lives get busier, the pressure to succeed, earn and spend increases. This means our resource-seeking system needs to be activated most of the day. The more this is activated, the more we seek, and the more failure, frustration, disappointment and self-loathing we feel because there is always more that we 'should' be getting or achieving.

We are exposed to constant news and social media posts, movies and games about wars, murders and violence. Our threat system can't distinguish between wars on our street and half a world away, or between realistic dangers and fictional ones. It also doesn't distinguish between real-life dangers and thoughts or memories about dangers. Our body can be activated when we hear someone shouting at us and also when we remember someone shouting at us or worry that someone might shout at us. Whenever there is a risk, whether immediate or imagined, near or far, our threat system activates. The more our threat system activates, the more anger, anxiety and disgust we are likely to feel.

If our resource-seeking and threat systems are constantly activated, then there is less time for our bodies to be in the soothing system, to restore internal balance and to feel calm. Some of us, especially those who are in stressful life situations, have traumatic pasts or constantly berate ourselves, may never have time or space to activate our soothing systems. Instead, our bodies feel like they're under constant threat or stress, and small frustrations or even neutral comments can be experienced as dangerous. Without time spent in our soothing system, we don't get to feel safe or content. Soothing is not just the absence of danger; it also includes the presence of comfort and support from others, having our needs met, being spoken to in a caring voice and having affectionate touch from others who care about us.

So we have these brains and bodies that are highly sensitive and reactive to signals of threat, but we have also inherited the antidote. Our brains have evolved to be soothed and settled by signals of care and compassion. This is what we are doing in this chapter, balancing our threat-sensitive mind by giving it exactly what it needs: the safety and confidence that comes from being cared for.

Since we're talking about cats, let's talk about my favourite cat: the tiger. Imagine you're lying on a beach on holiday. Your body relaxes, your brain thinks creatively and abstractly, imagining projects you might take on or are planning for the future, and you can think about a broad range of people and what's going on with them.

Then the news reports that a tiger has been seen on the loose in the city you're in. When you hear this announcement, you might not totally freak out yet because it's a big city, but you do become more alert. Your senses sharpen, and your thoughts become more concrete and practical. Rather than thinking about the past or future, your focus switches to the next few hours and where you and those you love need to be. Your sphere of concern reduces from the whole world to your specific community, thinking about the people you know and who might be near this tiger.

Suddenly, the tiger appears on the beach. Now any creative, flexible or reactive thoughts about the future or other people disappear. Your brain becomes less rational and more emotional, worried about the immediate safety of you and your closest loved ones. Your body prepares to run away by increasing your heart rate, tensing your muscles, making your breath quicker and sharpening your senses even more.

Then the tiger sees you and starts walking towards you. Your body's fight-or-flight instinct fully engages; heart pumping quickly, breath very shallow to get as much oxygen around your body as possible, muscles ready to run. Your brain focuses on the next few seconds and your own safety, relying on instincts.

(There is one final stage where the tiger is on top of you, ready to take a bite, and you have no chance of escape. At this point, your body slows down as much as possible, heart rate slowing to minimise blood loss, muscles relaxing to minimise tissue damage, senses dulling, and your brain distances itself from what's going on, not thinking at all. This is called dissociation and is very useful when a tiger is about to eat you, but very unhelpful when it continues after the threat has passed. Unfortunately, this ongoing state is common for people who experienced multiple childhood traumas that they could not get away from).

So, the more threatened you feel, the more your body tenses, the more your mind focuses on your immediate wellbeing, and you use short-term strategies. If you don't feel safe or content, you don't get to think creatively and abstractly to make bigger long-term plans from solid ground. Instead, you constantly find yourself reaching for short-term fixes, like alcohol, drugs, chocolate, avoidance, snapping at people, compulsions, procrastination and many others.

These are behaviours that you know won't help you in the long term, but when you're feeling under threat, you physically aren't able to think about the future. The more your threat system activates, the more your focus will be on getting yourself through the next few minutes or hours. This happens much more frequently and intensely for people who grew up in warzones or environments with violence or threats of violence. It can also happen frequently for people who did not receive enough love, care and validation or grew up in critical or unsupportive homes. It can also be more often for people who have strong emotions or talk to themselves in critical or invalidating ways. Examples of people who struggle with prolonged heightened states of fear include those who have experienced multiple traumas without support, those who come from marginalised groups or ethnicities with intergenerational trauma, and neurodivergent people. You might also struggle with this if you have a stressful job or home life, have poor sleep due to shift work or caring for young babies, or you spend too much time on your phone in the middle of the night.

There's a reason why we might give up on our diet and go back to junk food after a relationship break-up, find ourselves drinking or smoking when things go wrong at work, or snap at people when we have lots on our mind. Some of us even have thoughts about self-harm or suicide when life gets overwhelming because our brain is doing its job of looking for short-term solutions to escape from the painful stuff. In this heightened state, we are less able to think about more effective solutions, the needs of others, or to care about broader communities, humanity or the planet.

Hopefully, you're picking up on the importance of increasing your soothing system and cultivating compassion. Your threat system and resource-seeking system are useful, but if you can't also access your soothing system then you'll find it harder to catch your breath, to see the bigger picture and to generate more rational and long-term solutions.

Yet, even as we're discussing this, your resource-seeking system may be saying that you don't have time to do this and there are too many things to do, and your threat system might be warning you to skip this chapter because it doesn't feel safe to let your guard down even for a minute.

Notice those feelings if they're showing up, and observe that you're able to keep reading this chapter and try out the ideas, even while those feelings are there. That cautious part of you can warn you of dangers, without being the boss of you.

One of the most common things I hear when I work with people who are suffering is, *'Oh, it's not that bad, others have it much worse'*. They're suggesting that compassion is limited and giving any to themselves would take it away from someone else.

Here's the cool thing about compassion: it's not a finite resource. In fact, the more you give, the more there is. You can give compassion to everyone who needs it (spoiler alert: that's everyone, including you).

You can accept compassion from others without taking it from someone else who you think might be more deserving of it than you. Although I'm not sure what 'deserving of it' means, since when was compassion something that had to be earned? Additionally, allowing others to take care of you is a gift, as research suggests that people's wellbeing improves when they have the opportunity to be caring.

So, here's something to try: next time someone says something nice to you, rather than disagreeing with them in your mind or out loud, try saying 'thank you' and allow yourself to receive their care. Next time someone hugs you, see if you can permit yourself to lean in and accept their touch and their care.

You can give yourself compassion and accept that compassion from yourself without anyone else in the world having less.

How do you give compassion to others, accept compassion from others, and give and accept compassion from yourself?

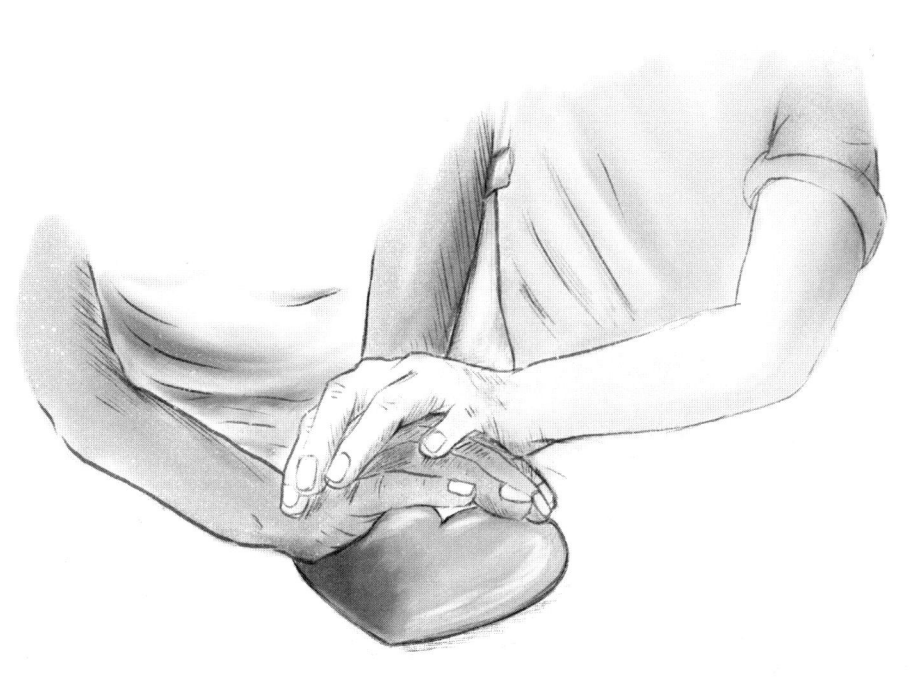

EXERCISE:
Flows of compassion

Bring to mind someone you care about. Imagine looking them in the eye and wishing them happiness, health, peace and care. Notice what it feels like inside you as you give them this compassion.

Then, imagine that person looking you in the eye and wishing you happiness, health, peace and care. Allow yourself to receive all that they're giving you. Notice what it feels like inside as you accept their compassion.

Finally, imagine looking yourself in the eye (or actually stand in front of a mirror and look straight into your eyes). Envisage wishing yourself happiness, health, peace and care. Notice how it feels inside as you give yourself compassion and accept compassion from yourself.

Reflect on that exercise. Which parts felt more natural? Which parts felt more uncomfortable? Were you able to experiment with giving compassion even while uncomfortable? Depending on all your experiences and interactions in life up until this point, you may have found all, some or none of that exercise comfortable or pleasant.

Chances are that you found some or all of the exercise challenging. Almost everyone gets blocked sometimes or struggles to give themselves compassion. You can be compassionate with yourself for finding it hard to be compassionate with yourself. Expect the compassion blocks, acknowledge them, and hold them gently. Fear or resistance to compassion exercises are normal. If it was that easy to constantly treat ourselves with compassion, we would all do it naturally with ease. But often allowing care into yourself awakens old memories of being in that care-seeking role in the past, where you might have been let down, frustrated, overlooked or actively hurt. Or it can feel foreign because you have never really experienced compassion towards yourself. If this is the case and you feel uncomfortable, sad, angry or lost when practising compassion, this is perfectly normal. After all, it's a new skill, and new skills take time to learn. Be patient with yourself, understanding that this means you need *more* compassion and *more* time with these soothing feelings to allow them to be helpful.

And despite all these understandable challenges, you tried it anyway.

Gosh, you are awesome.

Internal tone of voice

Let's say that someone you care about tells you that they're ready to learn to drive, and asks if you know any driving instructors. You think about who you know and realise that you know two different driving instructors.

Alex is tough and loves to get quick results. You'll hear their impatient tone when you are told to get it right. When you make a mistake, you are told that you're an idiot who should be able to do it already. When you get something right, the response is, 'About damn time, now don't make any more mistakes.' You get called a fool if you act confidently and much worse things if you act cautiously. You are frequently told that you might as well just give up, you'll never get the hang of driving. Yet if you consider listening to that advice and giving up, you get yelled at for being a quitter.

Sam, the second instructor, also likes results and sits alongside you and tells you that you are supported as you learn to drive. You are regularly reminded that learning to drive takes practice, and that everybody had to learn to drive at some point. When you make a mistake, you get ideas about how you could do it differently next time from a kind voice that encourages you to try again. When you get something right, it is acknowledged, especially when it is something that you had to practise a few times before getting it right. When it feels stressful or hard, Sam nods and says, 'It's OK to find it hard, learning to drive is hard and we can do it; let's try again.'

Which driving teacher are you likely to recommend to someone you care about? Would it be Sam?

How about if the person who wanted the recommendation wasn't someone you particularly cared about? Maybe it was your workmate's neighbour's cousin looking for a driving teacher. Which of these driving teachers would you recommend to this person you've never even met? Would it still be Sam?

How about for you? Which driving teacher would you select for yourself if you had to learn to drive? Hopefully Sam.

Which internal voice do you actually listen to on a daily basis?

If you're like me, and like most people I've spoken to, you'll have an internal voice who talks in a bullying tone, the way driving teacher Alex talks to their students.

Do you talk to yourself in a tone of voice that you would never consider using on a stranger, let alone someone you care about? Do you make a big deal about small mistakes you make, and then forget to acknowledge your successes? Do you tell yourself to give up and then admonish yourself for even considering giving up?

Does it help? Or does it make things harder?

Here's the weird thing about the bullying voice: it might be your biggest fan. It's the part of you that thinks you should be able to do anything and everything. The part of you that believes you can get it right the first time you do it. The part of you that thinks you should always say the right thing, present the right way, think the right things, feel the right things and so much more. The bullying voice wants the best for you, wants you to achieve it all. But its methods don't work.

The more it bullies you, the harder it is to do things that you would like to achieve in life.

Maybe your bullying voice tells you that things would be even worse if you treated yourself with compassion. My internal mean voice often tries that trick. It confuses compassion with giving up or laziness. Actually, when I do tune in to my compassionate voice, it still wants me to push myself, but it encourages me in a supportive way.

EXERCISE:
Compassionate voice

I invite you now to take in a breath . . .

And let it out . . .

Imagine for a moment that sitting alongside you is a really **kind** version of you. Or maybe you prefer to imagine that sitting alongside you is someone else who really cares about you. You can bring to mind someone who spoke to you with kindness or treated you with love. Maybe it was a parent or grandparent or teacher or coach. Or think of a character from a book or a film who talks with kindness or love. That kind person, whether it's you or another, sits alongside you, maybe even rubs your back.

Allow yourself to really listen to that kind voice. It sits next to you shoulder to shoulder and it's on your team.

What does this kind you or other person say to you?

What tone of voice does it talk to you in?

What does it feel like internally to listen to this **kind** part of you?

Maybe it says something like, *'I'm sorry that you're having to deal with this'*.

Take in another breath . . .

And let it out . . .

Now imagine that sitting alongside you is a really **strong** version of you. Or someone else real or imagined who represents supportive strength to you.

This **strong** voice is also on your team and wants you to succeed.

What does it say to you?

What tone of voice does it use when talking to you?

What does it feel like when you tune in to this strong part of you?

Can you hear it telling you that you can find a way to manage this challenge or hold this feeling?

Again, take in a breath . . .

And let it out . . .

This time, sitting alongside you is a really **committed**, confident version of you. Or someone from your life, or a book or movie, who reminds you that you can take steps towards the life that matters to you.

This **committed** voice has got your back and only wants the best for you.

What does it say to you?

What tone of voice does it use when talking to you?

What does it feel like when you tune in to this committed, confident part of you?

Maybe it can remind you of the importance of taking one step at a time. You don't need to fix everything at once, and every step helps.

And yet again, take in a breath . . .

And let it out . . .

This time, imagine that sitting alongside you is a really **wise** version of you or someone who represents wisdom for you. This **wise** voice can see a bigger picture and help you put things in perspective. And it's on your team.

What does it say to you?

What tone of voice does it use when talking to you?

What does it feel like when you tune in to this inner wisdom?

Can the wise voice remind you that it makes sense that you hurt based on where you've been, and that things can change?

One more time, take in a breath . . .

And let it out . . .

This time, imagine that sitting alongside you, shoulder to shoulder, is a **compassionate** version of you. Or someone else who represents compassion to you. This compassionate voice is

Kind
Strong
Committed
Wise

And they're on your team.

What does this compassionate voice say to you?

What tone of voice does it use when talking to you?

What does it feel like when you tune in to this compassionate part of you?

Maybe something like:

This is hard, you've got this

The compassionate voice can even talk to the bullying, critical part of you. Maybe it can say something like:

> Thank you for wanting to push me and get the best out of me
>
> and for expecting me to get it right perfectly every time,
>
> but your methods aren't helping.
>
> I've heard you, and I've got it from here.

So there are many parts to compassion.

Sometimes you'll need kindness, but other times kindness isn't so helpful. On those days, you need more strength or wisdom to push yourself compassionately to keep going and finish that task. For example, kindness might tell you that you're feeling awful and you should stay in bed or eat more junk food, whereas your compassionate voice might say, *'I get why you want to do that right now, and you'll feel better if we do some exercise or cook a meal or finish that piece of work.'*

Here's something to try next time you face a difficult task. And of course, different things will feel difficult to each of us on different days.

When it's time to tackle this task, notice what your inner voice says. Is it your compassionate voice, supporting you with kindness, strength, confidence and wisdom? Or is it your critical voice, putting you down for finding the task difficult, for not having dealt with it already, or for needing help with it?

Also, recognise that it doesn't need to be one internal voice or the other. The critical inner voice will still be there because it's been there for years and isn't going to just disappear. But maybe it no longer needs to hold the megaphone. Maybe you can notice that it's there while observing that there's also a compassionate voice you can choose to tune in to.

And if your inner critic is telling you that you don't deserve compassion, please notice that too. Is compassion something that needs to be earned? Do others need to deserve compassion? Or is it something you want to give to everybody, including yourself?

Tuning in to a compassionate inner voice can take a great deal of practice. **Some days you might need to give yourself compassion for finding it hard to give yourself compassion**.

Hopefully, over time, this voice will become more familiar and you can tune in to it quicker. But if you don't practise tuning in to it regularly (I recommend every day), then you can't expect it to be readily available on your hardest days.

This isn't a magic fix for the heavy things in your life, but the heavy things are hard enough without beating yourself up too.

Dalia sits in the bathroom crying, listing all the reasons why she has no right to feel sad or find life hard. She has listened to this album on repeat for years.

Then she pauses. She places her hand on her heart and takes in three compassionate breaths. She asks herself what she would say to a friend in a similar situation to hers and she noticed that she would never tell a friend that they had no right to feel sad. She experiments with talking to herself in a compassionate voice. It feels cheesy and forced but still she feels a tear on her cheek; a different kind of tear, a supportive tear. She gives herself a little hug and tells herself it's OK to find things hard and that she can do this one step at a time, breath by breath, minute by minute, until she feels able to manage hour by hour or even day by day.

Chapter Five.
Holding the Heavy Stuff with Curiosity

I hope you're starting to understand the importance of connecting to the present and talking to yourself in a compassionate way. And even with those skills, the Heavy Stuff is still there. Critical and judgemental thoughts about yourself, your past, your future, you appearance, your choices...

You're not alone with this. Most of us have minds that relish the opportunity to put us down. This is even more so for those of us who had to learn to blame ourselves as a survival tool when we were younger.

If you grew up in an environment where adults told you that you are no good or led you to feel like you don't matter, then it's often safer to believe them than to try to live in a world where you can't trust adults. If you told yourself that it's your fault, then maybe there's something you can do to make their behaviours stop. Maybe when you were growing up someone older than you did things to you that caused pain or felt uncomfortable, but then no one told you that what was done to you was wrong. When this happens, a child is left with a horrible choice, and it's usually automatic, not deliberate. The child can trust their own experience that what happened was wrong or they can numb out their own emotions and believe the adults who are supposed to keep them safe. The second option is a much better short-term survival option, even though it can lead to numbness, self-loathing or dissociation later on.

Even if you grew up in a completely supportive environment, where you only received love and support, your mind might still tell you that you should do more, do better or do it faster. We have all evolved to compare ourselves to others and this would have helped you succeed in some ways and feel disappointed in yourself at other times (maybe even at times when others thought you were succeeding).

It's likely that any judgemental or harsh beliefs you have about yourself developed for a reason, and it might still feel too hard and exhausting to try correct them now. Even if the specific thoughts you had were never helpful, the skill of comparing yourself to others and to imagined versions of yourself is a skill that evolved to help humans stay safe and move forward in life.

I've used the word *notice* a number of times in this book. That's because noticing is one of the most powerful tools you have. Noticing is the magic power you use to see all that's out there in the world and that helps you view the direction you want to go in. Without using your noticing power, you are trapped listening to a mind that tells you loads of heavy stuff, regardless of whether the heavy stuff is helpful or not. When you use your noticing power, you can observe your body and the actions you choose to take and see what happens when you take these steps.

Like all animals, humans have minds that are mostly focused on keeping us safe and they do it by being on the lookout for people or things that might hurt us. Our mind even wants to help us keep away from harmful emotions, memories and thoughts. As we've already discussed, trying to keep away from things that might hurt us is sometimes a really sensible idea, especially when the dangers exist in the outside world. At other times, it's the attempts to avoid things (especially internal things like thoughts and feelings) that keeps us stuck in our suffering.

But before I get too caught up in trying to explain things, let's get to know your noticing power.

EXERCISE:
Noticing from multiple angles

Take in a breath and observe what you are experiencing internally right now. What does it feel like in your mind and body in this moment? What thoughts, stories, feelings, judgements, memories, urges, images and sensations are showing up? Are you noticing that some are labelled as positive, some feel more negative and some feel neutral?

Now, in your mind's eye, imagine sitting in a chair across from you. Have a look back at you. You can't observe thoughts and feelings from this perspective, so notice what can you see from this angle.

Then, in your mind's eye, travel out of your window and keep going a few streets down, and from there look back at yourself sitting in the chair. What are you noticing as you watch yourself from this distance?

Finally, jump into your mind's eye's time machine and move forward ten years. From this point in the future, look back at the you sitting on your chair now. What can you see when you look at yourself from there?

I don't know what that experience was like for you, nor will I tell you what you should notice from any angle. Some people notice a lot of hurt, discomfort and negativity when they're observing themselves from where they're sitting but then see different things when they're looking back from different perspectives. Others really struggle to step outside their mind and look from other places.

Maybe when you looked at yourself from the chair opposite you, you could see that you are looking sad or worried? Or possibly you saw that the person you're looking at is more than those feelings?

When you looked at yourself from a few streets away, maybe you saw a human being who like all humans has thoughts and emotions and other internal experiences?

And when you looked back from the future, a whole myriad of emotions might have shown up. Possibly you saw someone sitting on a chair who could be achieving more? Or maybe you saw someone who is in the process of choosing to take steps to move their life closer to the life they want in ten years' time? Maybe future you is able to tell you that these steps are worth it?

It's difficult to describe possible experiences or thoughts you might have while trying that exercise without implying that there are 'correct' ways to respond. I promise you there is no correct way to see yourself from each of those places. For some people, the distance will help lead to more positive thoughts; for others, the exercise leads to more hurt or judgements.

But I'm hoping that, regardless of what you noticed, you were able to notice that you could notice. That you could see yourself from different perspectives – from places where you're really close to all the thoughts and feelings, and places where you can have some distance and observe other things.

It's the noticing that matters.

Because, if you can notice all these internal experiences and observe them from different perspectives, then you can notice that you're more than your thoughts and more than your 'I am' stories and judgements about yourself and others. This noticing allows for space and curiosity.

Rather than needing to correct every thought and judgement in your mind or figure out whether they are true or not, you can begin to see them for what they are – internal experiences that you can choose to listen to when they're helpful, or compassionately let them be there when they're not helpful.

You can hold the heavy stuff with curiosity.

In this book I don't want to try to 'fix' your thoughts or tell you that you've been thinking about things in the wrong way. If that critical part of your mind has spent years telling you that you're no good, then I'm sure you've already tried every possible argument you can think of to tell yourself that it's not true. I bet that every time you do this, your critical mind has blocked or resisted your counter-argument.

But what if you don't need to 'correct' your thoughts?

How about instead you curiously notice that they're thoughts? Thoughts can feel

heavy, huge, *true,* permanent,
and potentially even **lethal**

They can tell you that you'd be better off not being here.

And they are thoughts. Sometimes they're loud and specific. Sometimes they're more vague or menacing.

These thoughts developed to help you avoid short-term hurt. They came about to stop you doing things that might lead you to be kicked out of your tribe or experience social rejection. They may be thoughts that tried to stop you from being criticised, embarrassed, punished, assaulted. Thoughts that tell you that you'll be in a whole lot of pain or trouble if you don't treat everything your mind says as true and urgent.

These thoughts are amazing when they're helpful. But chances are, you hold onto them tightly even when they're not helpful. Then, because they're so painful, you spend lots of time and energy trying not to hold them, and you find yourself fighting back against internal experiences. You can't fix all these thoughts with arguing, distracting, ignoring or positive affirmations.

Now here's the exciting part. You don't need to fix these thoughts. You don't need to have every thought in your head be positive, supportive, optimistic, generous to yourself and others.

Instead, what if you noticed that thoughts are just thoughts?

EXERCISE:
I am...

For the next minute, listen to the thoughts showing up in your mind, or the ones that blast your mind on a bad day. Don't try to mute these thoughts or correct them. Instead, listen to them with curiosity. What your mind is saying may or may not be true – it may or may not be taken out of context or grossly exaggerated. For this exercise, let it say whatever it wants to say. Notice what it feels like to be listening to the stories that your mind hands you, and notice where you feel it in your body. Realise that you are here choosing to observe mental activity in your mind.

Then pick one of the mean thoughts that begin:

I am _____

Notice what it feels like as you listen to the 'I am . . .' story. The story that shows up on a bad day or when you make a mistake or for no particular reason.

Now with the same 'I am . . .' story, say:

I am noticing

that I am having a thought that

I am _____

What does this second sentence feel like compared to the first sentence?

What does it feel like to notice that you are listening to a thought?

If you are able to notice that you are having a thought, then you must be separate from that thought.

The thought may be true or false, it may be in context or maybe it's ignoring important facts.

Right now, the truth of it doesn't matter. You get to choose how much energy you put into struggling against that thought or, instead, you can let that mental activity be there while you put your energy into the people, things and ideas that matter to you.

Of course, mental activity isn't always easy-to-hear specific thoughts. Sometimes it can show up as an image or a vague feeling of unworthiness or shame. Maybe it shows up as an urge or a body sensation.

These are all internal experiences that can be wrestled with. Alternatively, these images can be observed with curiosity.

So, let's try a similar exercise with images.

EXERCISE:
Observing images

Can you bring to mind an image from the past or the future that causes distress when it shows up?

You don't need to start with the worst image; we all have lots of smaller uncomfortable images that we can try this with. Maybe a moment from the past when you did something you regret. Or an image of something going wrong in the future. I'm guessing it brings along some thought bodyguards that tell you it's not safe to look at this image, so you'll need to notice these are showing up too.

Bring that image to mind, and watch it. What does it feel like as you look at the image? Also notice the shame, worry, sadness or other uncomfortable feelings that show up too.

Image of a terrible thing happening

And then notice that it's an image. Maybe even place it in a frame or on a TV screen.

I'm noticing

that I'm watching an image of

a terrible thing happening

What does it feel like to notice that you are watching an image? Maybe it really happened, or maybe it might happen in the future. It probably feels awful to watch.

But right here, right now, you are able to notice that you're watching an image.

And you are more than that image. You are more than your worst days.

In a similar way, do you notice that you're having a brutal non-specific feeling that you're no good or to blame? Are certain urges and body sensations showing up?

It's not easy to just let those be there. It goes against so much of your learning history that you should do all you can to get away from things that hurt.

Noticing whatever is there is one of the most powerful tools you have.

Not to get rid of the heavy stuff, but to help you hold it, because we all have to hold heavy stuff.

I'm calling it the heavy stuff because it feels heavy. These painful thoughts, feelings, memories, urges, sensations and images don't just sit lightly inside you like candy floss. The heavy stuff weighs you down, affects your ability to eat, sleep, concentrate, feel connected to others and so much more. You have a thought or image in your mind, and you respond as if it is true and happening right now.

When you remember something scary happening in the past, your body responds as if you are in danger right now.

You imagine doing something embarrassing in the future, and you feel embarrassed right now as if it has already happened.

This ability to respond to thoughts or images as if they're true and happening right now is a very helpful skill in lots of situations.

When you're talking to a friend about a stressful event, you can feel more empathic and caring if you have a physiological response to their words. Imagine how much harder it would be to give them heartfelt caring if you could only use your mind to guess what they might be feeling.

Imagining feeling shame can prevent you from acting in foolish ways, even when your mind is still considering it.

When you're reading poetry or hearing song lyrics or are absorbed in a book, you can feel the emotions that the writer or the character is experiencing, even if it is far from your personal experience.

When you're watching a movie, you can feel worry or compassion for a character, such as a dragon or alien, even when you know rationally that they are just a computer-generated image. The movie fails if you're watching it but thinking about how good the CGI is rather than having an emotional response to the creature.

At other times, this same skill is unhelpful. You probably don't like people talking about vomit at the dinner table because it feels as gross as if there was vomit in the room. You might try not thinking about something that happened in the past because the emotions it generates right now feel too overwhelming. You might avoid doing something that matters to you because you've imagined it going wrong and the emotions you're feeling in this possible future are too painful. You might have thoughts that you are stupid, fat or a failure and then you feel awful. You might have an image of something terrible happening if you don't do something right, and then feel like you're responsible for this imagined event.

Unfortunately, you might even picture a future that is better off without you in it or imagine a death that is less painful than how you feel now and then want to die.

So this skill is sometimes helpful, other times not. You don't want to lose this ability, but you can benefit from noticing when it is keeping you stuck or getting in the way of you doing things that might move your life in directions that matter to you.

You can use your curiosity to notice that you're holding on tightly to a thought or an image and then choose to see what else is out there, find the people you want to be closer to and the adventures you want to have.

Erin noticed all the stories that had become so automatic to her that she didn't even realise she was listening to them. There was the *'everyone is judging me'* story, the *'I'm not good enough'* story and the *'I'm going to screw everything up'* story. She realised that it made sense that she would hold onto these stories tightly; her family had always valued success and appearing successful, which kept her constantly on the lookout for times that she might not be succeeding.

Then she noticed that these stories were actually making it harder for her to achieve the things she cared about, but arguing with them took lots of energy.

She imagined taking all these stories about herself that she had developed over her life and putting them in an imaginary book called *My Brain's Stories About Me*. Once they were in that book (with some blank pages left at the end for all the stories her brain was yet to write), she no longer felt so much pressure to get rid of the stories. Instead, she imagined putting that book in her bag and carrying it with her as she hung out with friends, did her best at work and began planning that overseas trip she'd been putting off. It felt uncomfortable having that book, but there was room for it in her bag. She could hold the heavy stuff.

Acceptance

We were raised to believe that life should be better than this – more fun, more successful, more comfortable, more cool stuff, less sadness, less worry, less bad stuff. We're given this message repeatedly – be good and good things come to you; work hard and you'll get what you deserve. Every ad promises happiness, every social media influencer promises success. Parents, teachers, religions and politicians all promise us that we should be able to get more if we work for it and deserve it.

Unfortunately, pain is part of life. Pain comes to all of us at different times, in different forms and different sizes. Often it feels awful or unfair. Pain doesn't only befall those who deserve it or have done bad things or haven't looked after themselves.

There are sensible things we can do to reduce pain. Painkillers help . . . except when they don't. Thinking positively helps . . . except when it doesn't. Exercise and nutrition are great things, but are no guarantee of a healthy, happy life.

Sometimes, it is the attempts to avoid pain that leads to more suffering. We might take medication, drink alcohol, go to therapy, avoid people, say positive affirmations, miss work or do mindfulness meditation and feel better briefly, only to find that the pain comes back, maybe even a bit stronger or louder.

Instead, we need to find a way to accept the thoughts we don't like, the feelings that hurt and the physical symptoms that cause discomfort. But acceptance is not simple.

Acceptance is a word that seems to be used everywhere now. Sometimes, it's used dismissively. People might tell you to just 'accept it', meaning 'suck it up', 'ignore it' or 'stop talking about it'. Others were taught to associate acceptance with surrendering, giving in or putting up with injustice. I'm sorry if you've had this experience.

Acceptance can also be confused with tolerating a feeling. You might tell yourself you can 'put up' with a feeling, as long as it doesn't get too intense or stick around for too long.

Other times people try to treat acceptance as a clever therapy trick. If you can just 'accept' this sadness or anxiety or trauma or chronic pain, then you won't have to have it any more. Wouldn't it be great if this were true – if you could just use acceptance as a tool to avoid accepting what you're feeling?

But acceptance isn't a trick or a technique. Acceptance is about genuinely making space for the heavy stuff that you're holding. In this book, we're talking about how to get better at holding the heavy stuff, not finding ways to put it down.

Why on earth would we want to learn to hold the heavy stuff? It's heavy. It hurts.

And right now, you have it whether you want it to be there or not (although I'm not making any statement about whether you will always have it).

So, let's use our curiosity and noticing skills to get to know our pain.

EXERCISE:
Getting to know your emotional discomfort

For the exercise on the following page, you might wish to read through all the instructions, then put the book down and try it.

This exercise might feel hard or weird or even scary. So, before you begin, look around and notice that if you are able to read this book right now, you are safe right now. Even if parts of you aren't feeling sure.

Take a breath.

As you breathe in, what does it feel like to be breathing in?

As you breathe out, what does it feel like to be breathing out?

Now have a look around inside your body. What feelings, emotions and sensations can you notice? Are there any that feel raw or uncomfortable? Let's spend some time with those. Don't try to remove or change them, but notice them with curiosity, like you've never felt these feelings before.

Where do these feelings sit inside your body? How big are they? Do they have a shape? Do they have a particular texture or colour? Are they jagged or smooth? Are they heavy or light?

As you observe these feelings, are you also able to observe your breath? Watch as your breath comes into your body, passes around the feelings wherever they are sitting, and goes out of your body again. Let your breath do whatever it needs to do to care for you and nourish you. Observe this for a few cycles of breath.

Your mind might tell you that there is no room inside you for these feelings.

Yet, what is your experience telling you right now? You can breathe around these feelings. There is room inside you for these emotions and sensations, even for the feelings that are uncomfortable and you really wish weren't inside you. Notice that your breath is able to pass around these feelings too. Keep coming back to your breath. You've got this.

Now I invite you to take a warm compassionate hand and place it on the part of your body that is experiencing these feelings. What does it feel like to have the feelings and to have the breath and to have the warmth and compassion? Observe both the feelings and the compassion as you breathe in and breathe out.

Then slowly, when you're ready, take three more breaths before bringing your focus back to the room.

After you've done that exercise, take some time to notice what it was like to do it. What was it like to observe your discomfort rather than fight it? To see the discomfort for what it is rather than to listen to your mind telling you that it shouldn't be there or that you won't cope if it continues?

Can you notice that there is room inside you for the heavy stuff? Even the heavy stuff you really wish that you didn't have to be holding? You are bigger and stronger that any of these thoughts, emotions, sensations, urges or memories. Knowing that doesn't stop it hurting, but maybe the awareness that you can hold it frees up some energy that you would have spent fighting it, and allows you to do things that matter to you.

EXERCISE:
Noticing more than your mind tells you

So far you have used your noticing power to observe what's happening in your mind and what you're feeling in this moment. Now it's time to see what else is going on.

What's happening in your body right now? Is it tired, hungry, stressed? Is your heart beating quickly or are you slumped over? Are you pacing with lots of energy? Or does every step feel exhausting?

Sometimes your mind can demand all of your attention when actually your body is giving you useful information about what you need and what you should do next. So, for this exercise, I invite you to do things with your focus on your body and your actions. Chances are your mind will try to distract you with thoughts about what you *should* be doing or comparisons to the past or to imagined futures. When it does, notice that your mind is doing what minds do and then turn your focus back to your body and your actions.

Possible ideas to try curiously:

> Move your body in ways it's not used to
> Eat something you don't normally eat
> Talk to someone you don't often talk to
> Walk somewhere you don't often walk
> Smell something you don't often smell
> Sit quietly at a pretty view
> Do something you've been avoiding

Next, do something you've done many times but do it with more awareness of your body and your actions. What does it feel like when you're doing it this time?

Notice what's happening in your body *before* you do this task and notice how you're feeling.

Notice what's happening in your body *while* you do this task and notice how you're feeling.

Notice what's happening in your body *after* you do this task and notice how you're feeling.

What have you learned about yourself from doing this task?

Notice the magic that comes with being curious.

Jeong observed his sadness and his numbness. It doesn't seem fair that everything feels so hard. But then he noticed that saying 'it's not fair' wasn't helping him. Sitting in his room until he felt better wasn't reducing his pain. In fact, it was often giving him more time focusing only on his discomfort.

He took in a compassionate breath, and asked himself what he was able to do today. He noticed that he was feeling tired, struggling to concentrate, and not motivated to do anything. His mind was telling him that these feelings would never pass. But he also noticed that even when he feels like this, he is able to do more than his mind is telling him.

Playing football felt like too much for today but he could message his friends and say hi. He couldn't tell them everything, but he could tell them he was feeling awful. He even allowed himself to accept their care when they sent it back in their messages. He noticed that he was sad, and he is more than his sadness. He can hold this feeling with compassion and love and then leave his room.

Chapter Six.
Holding the Heavy Stuff with Purpose

Sometimes, you just need to get away from danger. If you see someone scary, you might run away without any thought about the direction. The goal is to just get away from the threat. This is the best thing you can do for survival.

But, at some point, you'll need to catch your breath and think about where you want to go, as well as where you are running from.

Thoughts and feelings can hurt, so often people respond to these internal experiences as if they are dangerous. We all have instincts that want to get us away from pain. We all live in a world where we are constantly told that we shouldn't feel certain feelings or think certain things. People say, 'don't worry so much', 'get over it' or 'don't dwell on the past'. It makes sense that we try to get away from these feelings. But trying to avoid them takes time and energy and is only effective in the short term. The feelings and thoughts come back and we have to spend more time and energy trying to get rid of them, until we're trapped in cycles of avoidance or overusing a substance or self-criticism or shame.

As a psychologist, every day I work with people asking for help to get away from their internal pain. It could be their sadness, worries, self-loathing, traumatic memories, stress, shame, guilt or another feeling. They describe their pain and I can understand why they want to get away from it. Their pain sounds excruciating and crippling. At the same time, if they only know what they are trying to get away from, then they inadvertently move forward while looking at the threats behind them without a plan or direction. That's why it's vital to talk to them about what they care about.

You may get away from these thoughts or feelings using alcohol, avoidance or procrastination. Or maybe you use strategies such as exercise, therapy or meditation. All these things can help you make some good distance from what you're trying to get away from. But you are still looking behind you. You're still keeping track of what you don't want in your life and, while you do that, those things are still in control of your life.

You're not a vampire. You won't live forever. You don't have all the time in the world to do the things you want to do. This is actually a really good thing. If I was immortal, I would think about practising guitar and learning new languages and organising a beach clean-up and a thousand other things I would like to do; maybe I would even plan to do them. But I probably wouldn't get around to doing anything because what's the hurry? I can always do it tomorrow.

In this chapter, we're going to think about the direction you want to move in. Don't accept painful emotions or critical thoughts for the fun of it. Do it because there's only so much time in the day and time left in your life and you only have so much energy. Any time that you are putting into getting rid of internal experiences you don't want is time you don't have to spend moving towards the people, things and ideas that matter to you.

Instead, hold all the heavy stuff and carry it with you in directions that matter to you. Hold the heavy stuff with purpose.

Purpose?

Lots of pressure in that word. When you think about it, your mind might fill with 'shoulds'. You live in a world that is quick to tell you what you ought to care about. You may know your family's values, community's values, church's values or political party's values. Social media shows posts full of outrage at people whose values are different to yours. People can get shunned or cancelled for having differing opinions. So saying what you value can feel daunting; no one wants to be ostracised or kicked out of their group for not caring about the 'right' things in the 'right' way with the 'right' intensity.

Yet, there are many important issues in the world, and you can't care about them all with the same level of energy. The more stress or anxiety you're feeling, the smaller your sphere of concern becomes. You can think about the needs of everyone in the world when you're feeling safer and more stable. When you're feeling anxious, overloaded or under pressure, your attention focuses on the needs of your smaller circle – your family, friends or group.

If you can't care about everything all the time with an equal amount of passion, how do you know where to put your limited time and energy? If you try to be everything for everyone all the time, you'll achieve nothing for anyone.

So, let's explore what matters to you.

EXERCISE:
The perfect coffee

Take your mind back to a time when you had a perfect cup of coffee. Or tea. Or ice cream. Not perfect because the taste was perfect. Perfect because of where you were, who you were with, what you were talking about. A brief moment when things felt just right.

I remember one time; my partner and I were travelling in Spain. We took the cable car up a mountain in Barcelona to a stunning view overlooking the city and beyond. We sat at the top, drinking our coffee and talking about bigger plans for our life as well as enjoying all we were learning by being in a different country. I felt happy and excited about possibilities, and my body was relaxed. Just thinking about it now reminds me how much I value travel and trying new things – and, even more so, making plans with people I love.

Another time, I took my two-year-old daughter to a botanical garden. She wasn't so interested in the coffee, but I drank mine as she found a small stage in the corner of the park and sang songs, acting out the words as she sang. I remember feeling energetic and enjoying the feeling of being there. Taking myself back to this brief moment reminds me of the importance and the joy that comes with being really present with my kids (something that can be hard to do in this world with so many distractions).

Think about your perfect moment. Allow yourself to really lean into the memory and the emotions. There may be joy or calm, or there may be sadness or grief that the moment has passed. All emotions are welcome and all give helpful information about what is important to you.

What did you learn about yourself and what matters to you by taking yourself back there?

EXERCISE:
My own personal purpose

How do you let go of getting it right for everyone all the time, and instead tune in to your own heart? How do you know what matters to you and then find ways to take steps towards that?

Answer this:

Who is important to me?

(Take your time with this question, there will probaby be multiple answers.)

Who is on your list?

Specific people? Your parents, your partner, your siblings, your children?

Broader circles, too – your friends? Your colleagues? Your community? The groups of people you identify with?

Maybe there are some people you haven't met yet who still make the list – you might want to meet a new partner or make more friends.

Read over what you have written. What shows up for you?

Are you one of the people included on your list of names?

You probably wouldn't want to be the only person on your list, and at the same time what would it be like if you weren't on your own list at all?

Now take another breath and answer this question with as many answers as needed.

What is important to me?

(Take as long as you need, but try not to overthink this question. Try not to get pulled into the 'shoulds', just list the things that feel genuinely important to you in this moment.)

What's on your list for this question?

Maybe your list includes some of these things?

Work *Learning* Hobbies *Spirituality*

Community **Environment** Arts

Health *Music* **Social justice** **Animals**

Humanity Sport **Creativity**

Travel Trying new things Tradition

Independence **Culture** Sexuality

Being Listening Love

There may be other things too. Add those.

Read over what you have written and notice any judgements or feelings that show up.

Finally, ask yourself this question:

How do I want to be as I care for the people, things and ideas that matter to me?

Honest   Respectful   Curious   **Loyal**

Courageous   Compassionate   *Spiritual*

Reflective   Open   *Safe*   Flexible

Traditional   Faithful   Humorous   **Bold**

Present   *Kind*   Wise

Consistent   *Peaceful*   **Religious**   *Helpful*

Determined   *Grateful*   Independent

Loving

(Please don't feel limited to stay within the words I've suggested here. Find your own words – these are just starting points.)

Now time for the hard bit.

Reflecting on what things you want to move towards and how you want to be along the way isn't always a lovely fluffy experience. This reflection can invite in all kinds of emotions and judgements.

So take another breath. Have a look around inside. What thoughts and feelings show up for you as you reflect?

Pride   Shame   *Excitement*

Regret   **Frustration**

Energy   Self-loathing

Contentment   Guilt

Motivation   Hopelessness

These thoughts and feelings can be wonderfully motivating or really uncomfortable. They might make you want to do more or just give up and go back to bed and wait until you feel better. You can't live a valued life without also needing some compassion and acceptance.

You're making a commitment to carrying the heavy stuff as you take steps towards the people, things and ideas that matter to you. Your internal experiences don't dictate whether you move in these directions or not, but moving might be slower or less comfortable than your mind tells you it should be.

One of the lies that we're often told while we're growing up is that if we do the right thing we'll feel good and if we do the wrong thing we'll feel bad. Then we grow up and learn that this isn't true at all. Lots of things that are bad for us or clash with our values feel really good, and often doing the things that matter to us feels painful, lonely or risky.

And they can still be worth moving towards.

This is it.

You only get one short, complicated, confusing life. You'll never again be as young as you are now. It's time to figure out what you care about and to care about it.

What does it mean to care about it?

To really care about the things that matter to you – both on the days when caring feels pleasant and rewarding and on the days when it feels damn hard.

Caring requires action. It doesn't matter how much you care about something if you don't do anything.

It's the doing that shows you care.

It's the doing that makes a difference.

It's the doing that tells you that you're moving in the directions that you want to go.

If you don't know where you want to go, then it doesn't matter how far you move.

If you don't notice milestones as you move, then you don't know if you're moving.

So how do you know that you're moving in the right direction?

What are the milestones you pass along the way?

What are the steps you can take today that will move you closer to the people, things and ideas that matter to you?

Now here's the really cool thing about steps: **It doesn't matter the size of the step; what matters is the direction.**

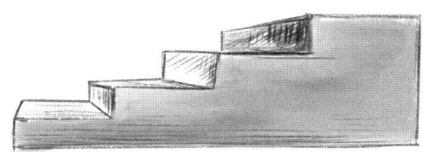

Some steps are huge – getting that career-defining job, your wedding day, completing a degree.

Most steps are small; sometimes so small that no one else can notice but you. These are the little things that you can do each day to help you move slightly closer to the life you want to be living. The extra five minutes with a family member; the page of study you get through; the message you send to a friend you haven't been in touch with for a while; the choice to say something compassionate to yourself . . .

Some people like to plan out their goals in advance. For example, you might say, 'Every day I'm going to run five kilometres,' or maybe, 'I will call my mother every week.' However, set goals can be hard to stick with, especially if you are feeling depressed, anxious, stressed or sore. This is particularly likely when you have selected a goal related to looking after yourself. They are usually the first goals to get dropped when people feel overwhelmed or stressed.

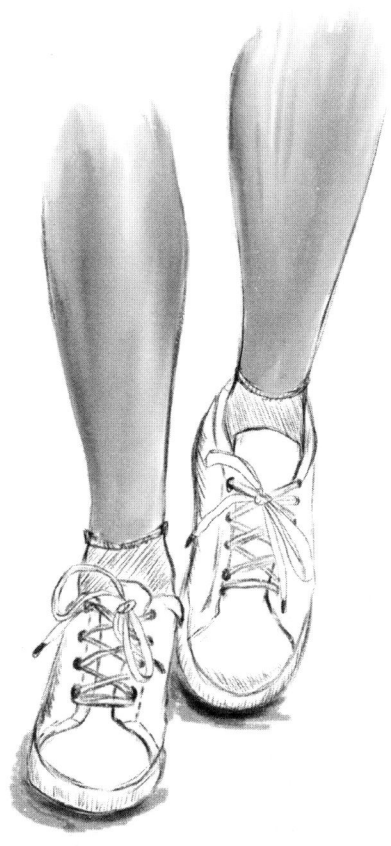

EXERCISE:
Stepping
Part 1: One step

Ask yourself:

'Given how I'm feeling today, what is one extra step I can take today that will bring me a little bit closer to what matters to me?'

If you are like most people, the way you feel and what you think you are able to do may vary from day to day.

Some days you might be feeling so low that brushing your teeth feels like an achievement.

Other days, brushing your teeth is just something you do on your way out of the house. And on those days, starting a conversation with someone or trying something new or returning to something that has slipped away might feel like an achievement.

Although the steps will differ, each day you can move a small distance in a direction that matters to you.

And each day your mind is likely to hand you reasons why that step is too hard or not the right thing to do or not the right day to do it. So there's more to this exercise:

EXERCISE:

Stepping
Part 2: Taking the step

Thinking about the step you picked for today, rate it out of ten.

Ten means you will definitely do it.

Zero means you'd love to do it, but let's face it, there's no way it's actually going to happen today.

What number did you pick?

What can you do to make it one number higher?

Here are some ideas:

Pick a specific time to do it.

Tell someone you're planning to do it.

Listen to others about what they're hoping to do. Support each other.

Plan a reward for after you've done it.

Find a friend to do it with.

Set a reminder on your phone.

Remind yourself why this step matters to you.

Imagine you on the other side of this step.

Talk to yourself with self-compassion rather than bullying yourself to do it.

Pick steps that are cross-off-able and can be achieved in the time you have.

Pick steps that can be measured so you know you've done them.

Say 'well done' to yourself after you've taken a step (even when you don't get the outcome you were hoping for).

Remember that really small steps can get you moving.

Bring to mind someone who believes you can do it. Have them in your mind as you do it.

If you can't get the number over seven, then pick a different step, because you probably won't do the one you initially chose.

It's better to take a small step than not get around to taking a larger step.

EXERCISE:

Stepping

Part 3: Taking the step

~~~~~~~~~~~~~~~~~~~~~~

At the end of the day, write down your steps for that day and which direction they are helping you move towards. Or look in the mirror and say them to yourself.

Some days, this part of the exercise may be harder than actually taking the steps.

Your mind may hand you thoughts such as:

'that didn't count'

or

'that wasn't big enough'

or

'you could have done more'

or

'you're pathetic for even needing to do this exercise'.

Minds can be so mean sometimes.

Even as your mind hands you those thoughts, are you able to write down your achievements anyway?

Can you treat yourself with compassion?

One more thing you'll notice about steps.

Every time you're taking a step towards something that matters to you, you're not able to take a step towards something else that matters to you.

For example, I really value my job. I love that I have the opportunity to sit with people and help them find space for their pain and then live a more valued life.

But I also really value my family. And my friends. And my community. And my health. And my planet. And music. And learning. And other things too.

I can only do one thing at a time. Every time I'm doing something, I'm failing to do something else that matters to me. I'm not available for my kids because I'm working, or I'm not able to catch up with my friends because I'm doing community work. And so on.

So even if I could live a life filled only with valued steps (which, of course, I don't), I'd still experience sadness, worry, regret and shame. There's no option when I don't ever have to hold some heavy stuff.

EXERCISE:
Stepping
Part 4: Reflection

Have a look at your list of things that matter to you.

Which are the ones you want to take a step towards every single day?

Which are the ones that you don't want to go a week without taking a step towards?

Which are the ones that you want to step towards at least once a month?

Which are the ones that matter to you, but, given the pressures on your time, might only get smaller steps this month?

 **Omar** sat at their desk, miserable at the thought of even having to open their inbox and read all the demands on them. Their parents told them that they're in their dream job. Five years ago, they would have thought this was their dream job. But now corporate law wasn't where their heart was. They thought about all the other types of law they could do that might satisfy them more – human rights, environmental law, supporting migrants.

These were all good causes, but Omar realised that they'd still have to be a lawyer and that wasn't who they wanted to be. It was time to find a way to do something more creative. It was time to start planning the scary career change to retrain as a graphic designer.

They started making a plan of how they could save enough money in the next twelve months so that they could afford to become a full-time student again in a year's time. They also bought themselves a sketch pad and decided to draw one illustration each day in the meantime. These plans felt daunting, but not nearly as terrifying as staying on this career path for the rest of their life.

Chapter Seven.

Holding the Heavy Stuff with Support

This world is a tough place. And it can feel like it's getting tougher. You can actively care for yourself and still struggle.

You are too important to hold all the heavy stuff alone without support. In fact, support from social connections may be the most crucial component of positive mental health.

In this chapter, we'll discuss the people who can help you and the lifestyle choices that can make a huge difference to your psychological wellbeing.

Community

In this scary, difficult world we are often told that the best way to survive and to get ahead is to be independent or to compete with each other.

That is simply rubbish.

None of us can do this alone. None of us can be happy or successful or live meaningful lives without other people.

Think of all the people you know who you would like to have in your life. Notice that each of them is a human being like you. A human being with hopes and fears and passions and dislikes. A human being who has had good days and bad days. A human being who gets it right sometimes and screws up sometimes.

None of these people are perfect at everything. Some say the right thing when you're struggling, others say things that miss the mark completely or make you feel worse. Some are really good at helping when you need a solution or a favour, others might add to your stress. The people you reach out to when you need help moving a lot of heavy boxes might not be the same people you reach out to when you are struggling to hold lots of internal heavy stuff.

Figure out who you can reach out to. Think about when is the right time to reach out to them. Plan the best way to reach out to them. At times of stress and anguish, it is common to try to let people know that you're struggling, but to do it in unhelpful ways, such as snapping at them, isolating yourself or reaching for those risky short-term strategies. But are there more effective ways you can let people know that things are feeling rough? Are there ways you can let them know what you need?

For example, is there someone you can message and say 'I'm having a hard time right now',

Can I talk about it?

or

Can I have a hug?

or

Can I have some fun distraction?

Hopefully you have people who can understand that you're having painful emotions, but don't see you as broken. People that can see you're having a hard time and give support rather than give advice or lectures.

I know not everyone has people in their life like this. Some people try to get support from people who aren't able to give it to them. I'm sorry if that's your current situation. I hope that, at some point soon, you find people who can give you meaningful support.

Because trying to hold the heavy stuff alone is ten times harder.

Professional support

Unfortunately, for so many people, trying to find a therapist adds to stress rather than reducing it. Therapists can be expensive and hard to find, and it can be confusing to know what type of therapist is the right fit for you.

If the ideas in this book resonate with you, then you might like a therapist who offers acceptance and commitment therapy (ACT). With an ACT therapist, you'll learn ways to hold the heavy stuff and carry it with you rather than sitting with someone who sees you as broken and wants to fix you.

But the type of therapy that the therapist offers is less important than whether they feel like someone **you can talk to** about stuff that can be uncomfortable, embarrassing or involves saying things that you haven't yet got words for. Does this person create enough space for you to talk about the thoughts and feelings you're struggling with and really take the time to understand your context – where you are now and where you've come from?

On the other hand, someone who just listens to stories you've already told yourself without helping you try something new may not be useful either. Your therapist should be asking questions or noticing things that help you learn new things about yourself and what you can try next.

It's really important that you and your therapist have the same goal for therapy. If you want to talk about your sadness and they want to talk about your drinking, then you're not going to get very far unless you can discuss why these things connect and have a shared agreement of what you're hoping to achieve.

There are lots of different types of people in the world, and there are lots of different types of therapists and therapies in the world. No one therapist and no one therapy is right for every person at every time. If the person you're talking to doesn't feel like the right fit for you or the type of therapy they're offering doesn't feel like it's matching your needs and goals, then talk about it with them or look for someone else.

Medication

We have a health system in which it is easier and cheaper to access psychiatric medications than it is to access therapy. This means that many people are offered antidepressants before they're offered a chance to talk about what's going on for them. This makes me sad.

I recommend finding a doctor who really listens to your experience and goals and is willing to explore different options with you. Just like therapists, it's OK to go to a new doctor if you feel you aren't being listened to and your opinions aren't being respected.

Some people find medication very helpful, but lots of people are putting up with side effects that can cause real discomfort in their life – sleep difficulties, weight gain, sexual difficulties, terrifying vivid dreams, sedation, even increased thoughts about suicide. If you do try medication, listen to your own body and your own experience and notice what the medication is actually doing rather than just hoping it will do whatever your doctor tells you it will do. Doctors know what medication does for other people, but you know what the medication is doing for you alone and it is important that you and the doctor work collaboratively.

Similarly, if you try medication and then decide to come off it, please do it in consultation with a doctor, because it needs to be done really gradually. I've worked with many people who tried to come off antidepressants too quickly, felt awful, and then assumed that they would need to stay on the medication for life. Later, when they came off the medication more gradually and used the ideas that they'd learned in therapy, the process went better.

Sleepertunity

Sleep is important. People who don't sleep enough are more at risk of depression, suicidal thoughts and impulsive behaviours. It's also harder for them to plan, concentrate and complete valued steps that help mental health.

But sometimes it can be hard to sleep. It is especially difficult to sleep when you're worried. It can be easy to fall into a cycle where you worry about not sleeping or what tomorrow will be like if you don't get enough sleep tonight, which then makes it harder to sleep.

You can't control if you sleep or not.

But you can control the things that you do that make it more likely that you might sleep. I call this sleepertunity: the things you can do to increase the chance that you'll have the opportunity to sleep.

Start with the basics.

Sleep routines are important. Let your body know that there are times when you should be awake and times when you should be asleep. You can do this by going to bed at around the same time each night and getting up around the same time each morning. Ideally, you'll roughly maintain this routine on weekends too.

In your last hour before sleep, do things that let your body know that it's time to get ready for sleep. Avoid large meals, alcohol, caffeine, cigarettes. Reduce bright lights – human brains developed before electric lights, when the only light was the sun. So our bodies know to be more alert when there's light and more sleepy in the dark.

This includes screens, especially phones. Try listening to an audiobook or reading a paper book before bed rather than being on your phone until right before you try to fall asleep. In particular, reduce games as these are designed to wake your brains up and make you more alert.

Bodies are wired to sleep when it is cooler and quieter and be more awake when the sun warms things up and more things are happening. So aim to keep your bedroom quiet, cool and dark.

Relaxing activities before sleep can also be helpful – a bath, a cup of herbal tea or a breathing exercise. These things let your body know it's time to prepare for sleep. Make sure that you get some time outside each day and do something physically active. Your body needs to know there are times to be awake. Exposure to bright light in the first hour or two after waking is a great way to strengthen your body's clock, helping with sleep later in the day. The best form of bright light is outside – even on a cloudy day, ten minutes is helpful.

Finally, if you find yourself lying in bed trying to fall asleep and you are getting more and more stressed or agitated about not being asleep, then get up and leave your bedroom. You don't want your bed to feel like a place that stresses you out. Even a short break from bed to walk around a little and have a drink of water can create a reset to go back to bed and see if sleep follows you.

If you find yourself awake, but are still relaxed and calm, then stay in bed. You're still getting some rest even if you're not actually asleep.

Learning to sleep for long enough at the right times takes practice, just like any other skill you want to learn. If it's not happening for you straight away, keep practising, maintaining a sleep routine that works for you, and focus on the things that you can do something about.

Food

The more stressed you are, the more you are likely to seek short-term solutions. This can be very true for your diet too. When you are sad, worried, stressed, angry or agitated, you might find yourself craving sugar or fats, and reach for the junk food or the treats. This gives you a brief hit that can help you feel better momentarily and then much worse after.

Choosing to eat healthier food, drinking more water and reducing the quantity and frequency of highly processed sugary and fatty foods is likely to have a significant impact on your mental health. The increased vitamins and minerals you get in more natural food will make a difference along with the psychological impacts of treating yourself with compassion by taking care with what you eat.

Don't try to radically change your entire diet, because even if you can, chances are the changes won't last. Instead, make one small step to turn your diet into more how you'd like it to be. Eat a varied diet, with more fruit and vegetables. Reduce one item that seems to end up on your plate more often than you'd like. Experiment to see if you feel any different if you make small changes to your diet.

This can be hard to do but science shows that diet matters.

Physical exercise

How do you feel after exercise? More focused? Confident? Stronger?

Life is so busy and finding time for exercise can be really difficult. You know yourself and you know what is possible for you. But the evidence is pretty clear; exercise is good for your mental health as well as your physical health.

See if you can add some more movement into your week. Notice what happens when you do a bit more exercise.

When you get really busy, it can be easy to drop exercise because it feels like something has to go and all other commitments feel more important. Finding a way to maintain exercise, even when you're busy, is an act of compassion. You are making a statement that you are one of the people on your list that you care about.

Hopefully you can find a way to make exercise not feel like a chore, but instead be rewarding for you.

It is also important to make sure that you look after your body in other ways too.

Do stretches

Adjust how you sit and stand to better suit your body's needs

Take your prescribed medication

See your doctor when you have health concerns

And of course, remember to breathe

Reducing alcohol and drug use

Are there toxins that are getting in the way of you living the life you want to live? Would it be easier to be the kind of partner, parent, friend or human you want to be if you were drinking less or using other drugs less?

There are all sorts of substances that help us feel better in the short term, or at least give us hope that maybe this time they'll help us feel better. The more alert our nervous system is (due to current and past stressors), the more likely we are to reach for short-term fixes.

But it can be really important to step back and notice the effects your alcohol or drug use is having on your health, your mood, your relationships and your ability to achieve other things that you want to be doing.

Reducing social toxins too

The same risks apply to social toxins. Social toxins might be face-to-face or online.

Identify places where you spend too much time, even though you know they're not good for you. Notice the times when you are surrounded by groups of people who seem to bring out the worst in you or leave you feeling wrong.

We know the importance of committed action and taking steps towards things that matter to you. But doom-scrolling does not help. Recognise if you are engaging in discussions that add to your frustration and outrage without helping you or anyone else.

There are companies making lots of money by sending you to links and feeds that increase your outrage (these companies know that you're more likely to reach for short-term strategies such as spending money when you're feeling agitated or unsafe).

Notice the places and people that take a toll. Choose how much time and energy you want to give. You can be in control.

Please, listen to your own body.

Choose to do what you need to care for yourself so that you can breathe, notice where you are right now and move towards the people, ideas and things in life that matter to you.

Tony looked at the calendar. How had another year passed? He had avoided all the stress and pressure that his friends had been dealing with, but still something felt missing in his own life.

He looked around the room; what did he have to show for the past twelve months? He realised that he didn't want to be in the same position in twelve months' time.

He still didn't know what he wanted to do with his future and felt anxious even thinking about it. But he had to admit that avoiding everyone and everything was beginning to feel boring too.

He looked through his cupboard and found his old running shoes. Hard to believe that he used to be a good runner. He knew that even though the first few runs would be hard, it wouldn't take too many weeks until he was an OK runner again. Especially if he got up at 9am instead of at noon, and if he held off smoking weed and eating junk food until the evening.

He also messaged a friend and suggested they meet for a coffee down by the beach rather than meeting online to game. He didn't know what to do next, but it was time to look after himself enough so that he could get his life moving again.

Holding stuff

Throughout these pages, we have discussed how we are all holding stuff that feels heavy – painful emotions, critical thoughts, bullying stories, horrific images, overwhelming urges. We noticed that everyone's behaviour and struggles make sense once you understand where they've come from and how they were treated in the past.

We observed how so much of our suffering is due to trying to get rid of those thoughts and feelings we don't want. The strategies we use to drop the heavy stuff work short term, but in the long term leave us holding more and more and feeling worse about ourselves and more despondent about our future.

So, instead, we learned how to hold the heavy stuff. We hold it one breath at a time, giving ourselves compassion as we do so. We talk to ourselves like we'd talk to a loved one – *'This is hard, and you've got this.'* We use our curiosity to see thoughts and feelings for what they are: internal activity that can observed, rather than needing to be fought. We turn our energy from resisting thoughts and feelings, and instead choose to take steps towards the people, things and ideas that matter to us. We look at other lifestyle factors and support systems that help us as we move in our valued directions.

As you've read this book and tried the exercises, hopefully you've noticed that you can hold more heavy stuff. Maybe along the way you've learned that it wasn't as heavy as your mind was telling you it would be. You may have observed that you are stronger and can hold more than your mind was telling you that you can hold.

Maybe it's still heavy, and yet carrying it is worth it because trying to get rid of all those thoughts and feelings is taking up time and energy that can be spent being the person that you want to be.

Whatever you have learned, I want you to know that **you are awesome**.

Just by reading this book, you have made a statement that you matter and deserve some self-care. Change is possible and in your grasp.

Thank you for giving me the gift of your attention.

Further Reading

Gilbert, P. & Choden (2013). *Mindful Compassion*. Robinson. This is a lovely introduction to compassion focused therapy, which has been so helpful in my practice and in my life.

Harris, R. (2022). *The Happiness Trap: How to Stop Struggling and Start Living* (2nd Ed). Robinson. This was the book that first helped me explain ACT ideas without jargon.

Hayes, L. L., Ciarrochi, J. V. & Bailey, A. (2022). *What Makes You Stronger: How to Thrive in the Face of Change and Uncertainty Using Acceptance and Commitment Therapy*. New Harbinger. The DNA-V model described in this book was first developed for teens, but has been wonderfully adapted here to help adults too.

Hayes, S. C. (2019). *A Liberated Mind: How to Pivot Toward What Matters*. Penguin. This book is by the man who first developed ACT, but it shows where ACT is going next.

Rucklidge, J. J & Kaplan, B. J. (2021). *The Better Brain: How Nutrition Will Help You Overcome Anxiety, Depression, ADHD and Stress*. Harvest. This book gives me so much hope for the future of mental health – the world needs to understand the role of nutrition in how we function.

Sedley, B. (2015). *Stuff That Sucks: Accepting What You Can't Change and Committing to What You Can*. Robinson. This is me presenting similar ideas to those in this book but targeted at teens.

Sedley, B. & Coyne, L. (2020). *Stuff That's Loud: A Teen's Guide to Unspiralling when OCD Gets Noisy*. Robinson. It was such a joy to co-write this book with Lisa, and it has been very rewarding hearing that it has helped teens all around the world struggling with OCD.

Walser, R. (2021). *The Heart of ACT: Developing a Flexible, Process-Based, and Client-Centered Practice Using Acceptance and Commitment Therapy*. New Harbinger. If you're a clinician, this book will help you offer therapy with more reflection and compassion.

Wilson, K. G. & DuFrene, T. (2010). *Things Might Go Terribly, Horribly Wrong: A Guide to Life Liberated from Anxiety*. New Harbinger. This book introduces ACT with so much compassion and fun, written for people struggling with anxiety or worries – in other words, everyone.

Winfrey, O. & Perry, B. D. (2022). *What Happened to You?: Conversations on Trauma, Resilience, and Healing*. Bluebird. This book is a summary of decades of research on the ways childhood trauma can affect brain development, but it's written in a way that is easily accessible to all.

Acknowledgements

Firstly, I want to thank every single client and family I have worked with. Thank you for trusting me and teaching me so much.

The acceptance and commitment therapy community is one of the most generous and caring communities I have ever been part of. I am so grateful for having the opportunity to learn from attending workshops or reading books by so many amazing people, including Sonja Batten, Tobyn Bell, Yvonne Barnes-Holmes, Lisa Coyne, Paul Gilbert, Russ Harris, Louise Hayes, Steven Hayes, Russell Kolts, Joe Oliver, Dennis Tirch, Laura Silberstein-Tirch, Matthieu Villatte, Robyn Walser and Kelly G. Wilson.

All their knowledge contributed to the ways I presented ACT in this book. Some of the exercises and metaphors in this book I have learned from specific people, and I am so grateful. Louise Hayes taught me about the importance of the 'noticer'. The 'compassionate voice' exercise was adapted from a workshop by Dennis Tirch. The 'driving instructor' metaphor comes from Russell Kolts (although he talked about tennis coaches). Lisa Coyne shared with me the 'perfect cup of coffee' exercise and the 'connecting with all of yourself' exercise. The 'noticing from multiple angles' exercise was adapted from a workshop by Steven Hayes. There is an exercise similar to 'getting to know your emotional pain' in *The Happiness Trap*. The 'tiger' metaphor for trauma came from a workshop by Bruce D. Perry.

I am also very lucky to be part of a supportive ACT community in New Zealand, including Giselle Bahr, Kerry Makin-Byrd, John Moffat and Kathryn Whitehead. Plus some support from some wonderful people across the ditch in Australia, including Julie Grove, Eric Morris, Linda Nicholson, Tiffany Rochester, Louise Shepherd and Jodie Wassner.

Thank you to my publisher Andrew McAleer, and everyone who read a draft and provided feedback, including Giselle Bahr, Tobyn Bell, Geraldine Eagle, Ngahuia Eagle, Louise Hayes, Dion Howard, Kerry Makin-Byrd, Claire Murdoch, Tiffany Rochester and Bronwyn Sweeney. Thank you to the amazingly talented designer Catherine Adam and illustrator Kalos Chan, you have made this book sing.

Finally, thank you to my incredibly wonderful friends and family. Thank you for being you and for being in my life .